Issues in Action

MASS INCARCERATION, BLACK MEN, AND THE FIGHT FOR JUSTICE

Cicely Lewis

Lerner Publications ◆ Minneapolis

LETTER FROM CICELY LEWIS

Dear Reader,

When I was five years old, my father was sent to prison. We wrote each other letters. One day, though, I got angry. Ashamed to tell people where my father was, seeing my mother struggle to pay bills—I felt betrayed by him. I decided I wasn't going to write him anymore.

Cicely Lewis

By the time he was released, I had moved on with my life. But when I stumbled upon a book about mass incarceration, I developed a new understanding. I realized that my father needed rehabilitation, not imprisonment. My father was a victim.

At the age of forty, I reunited with him. My father told me that he had wanted to reach out to me and that he had prayed for this day to come. My twelve-year-old son cried because he couldn't imagine not being able to see his father daily. Seeing him cry made me relive the pain and sadness that I had buried.

I hope this book can help bring reform to our justice system and save a family from the pain my family has suffered. I hope it helps you as a reader to better understand the effects of mass incarceration.

—Cicely Lewis

TABLE OF CONTENTS

Some of Isaac Wright Jr.'s legal arguments eventually formed the basis of new laws.

FREED FOR LIFE

IMAGINE BEING CONVICTED AND SENTENCED TO LIFE FOR A CRIME YOU DIDN'T COMMIT. You decide to study the law and win your freedom. Along the way, you successfully work to overturn the convictions of over twenty other inmates.

This story really happened. In 1991 Isaac Wright Jr. was convicted and sentenced to life in prison. He studied law in prison and oversaw his own appeal. Years later, Curtis

"50 Cent" Jackson, a rapper and TV producer, brought Wright's story to the screen. The series *For Life* debuted on ABC in February 2020. It aimed to raise awareness about inequalities in the criminal justice system. Sadly, Wright's story is true for many Black men in America—and many do not have a Hollywood ending. Black men have the highest incarceration rate of any group in the US.

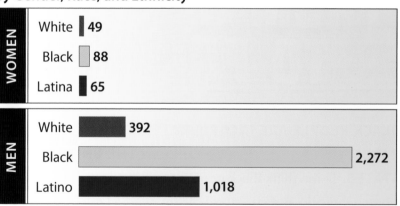

Rate of Imprisonment per 100,000, by Gender, Race, and Ethnicity

WOMEN
- White | 49
- Black | 88
- Latina | 65

MEN
- White | 392
- Black | 2,272
- Latino | 1,018

Source: E. A. Carson, "Prisoners in 2018," Washington, DC, Bureau of Justice Statistics, 2020.

Black men are incarcerated at almost six times the rate of white men. Black women are incarcerated at nearly twice the rate of white women.

Black men are more likely to be arrested and convicted than white men, and receive longer prison sentences.

CHAPTER 1
FROM SLAVERY TO PRISON

BLACK PEOPLE ARE INCARCERATED AT MUCH HIGHER RATES THAN ARE WHITE PEOPLE IN THE UNITED STATES. Some think Black people commit more crimes than white people do. But structural racism plays a large role in who is charged with crimes, who is convicted, and how long someone's sentence is.

The high rate of incarceration among Black people has deep roots in slavery. The first enslaved Africans arrived in the Americas in 1619. Enslaved people were forced to work on plantations under harsh conditions. They were deemed inferior by white people, who denied enslaved people the ability to vote, get an education, or own land. Enslavers separated people from their families and forbade them to travel. Enslaved people were traumatized by the effects of slavery. Even after slavery ended, echoes of slavery continued to appear in US law and policy for generations.

Frederick Douglass escaped from slavery in 1838 and became a leader in the abolitionist movement.

After the Civil War (1861–1865), the Thirteenth Amendment was added to the US Constitution to make slavery and involuntary servitude illegal. But it had one notable exception: slavery was illegal "except as a punishment for crime whereof the party shall have been duly convicted." This allowed white lawmakers, police, and judges to punish Black people with forced labor, effectively maintaining slavery under another name. During Reconstruction (1863–1877), white people in power leased incarcerated Black people to private organizations such as railroad and mining companies. After Reconstruction ended in the South, states expanded the practice of convict leasing.

> **"The United States has the highest rate of incarceration of any nation on Earth . . . central to understanding this practice of mass incarceration and excessive punishment is the legacy of slavery."**
>
> —Bryan Stevenson, founder of the Equal Justice Initiative

The end of Reconstruction also birthed another form of oppression: Jim Crow laws. These laws drew upon black codes that were passed after the Civil War and repealed during Reconstruction. Jim Crow laws were passed around the South to keep Black and white people separate as much as possible.

JUNETEENTH

The Emancipation Proclamation announced that slavery would end and that all enslaved people would be freed on January 1, 1863. But news traveled slowly in the nineteenth century. More than two years later, on June 19, 1865, Union soldiers arrived in Galveston, Texas. Only then did the state's enslaved people hear they were free. The celebration that followed inspired the holiday of Juneteenth. Many Black Americans continue to celebrate Juneteenth as the day slavery truly ended.

Performers at a Juneteenth parade in Philadelphia, Pennsylvania, in 2019

Slavery lived on through chain gangs, groups of incarcerated Black people leased out cheaply to work.

For example, Black people were forbidden from using the same drinking fountains as white people and were forced to ride in the backs of buses. Many of these laws were upheld far into the twentieth century.

Though slavery ended, white people continued to torture, abuse, and disenfranchise Black people by creating unfair systems, especially in the South. Practices such as convict leasing and Jim Crow laws were created not only to keep Black people in poverty but also to incentivize imprisoning them as a source of cheap labor. These practices and laws continued the legacy of slavery.

President Richard Nixon claimed drugs were the biggest danger facing Americans in a 1971 speech.

CHAPTER 2
UNFAIR SENTENCES

IN THE 1970S, PRESIDENT RICHARD NIXON BELIEVED THAT TOUGHER CRIME LAWS WERE THE BEST WAY TO DECREASE CRIME. Nixon was also deeply concerned about drug use. He began what became known as the War on Drugs. During Ronald Reagan's presidency (1981–1989), incarceration rates increased dramatically, especially for drug charges. But imprisoning more people did not decrease the crime. Instead, it led to mass incarceration, or the US imprisoning people at very high rates.

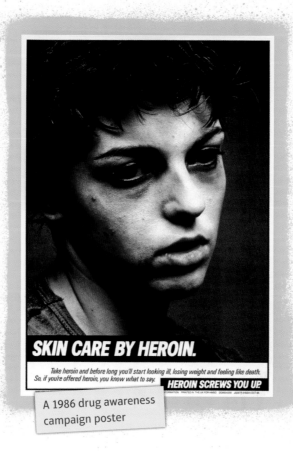

SKIN CARE BY HEROIN.

Take heroin and before long you'll start looking ill, losing weight and feeling like death. So, if you're offered heroin, you know what to say.

HEROIN SCREWS YOU UP

A 1986 drug awareness campaign poster

The War on Drugs became another way to criminalize and control Black people. Though Black people are not any more likely than white people to use drugs, they are more likely to be arrested and incarcerated for drug use. They also receive longer prison sentences.

During the War on Drugs, politicians who wanted to appear tough on crime supported laws that created mandatory minimums and classified drug charges as felonies. Mandatory minimums require a judge to sentence somebody for a minimum amount of time, often several years.

MASS INCARCERATION AND DISENFRANCHISEMENT

Laws created during the War on Drugs raised many drug charges to felonies, a more serious crime. In many states, receiving a felony conviction means you lose your right to vote, even after you are released from prison. In 2020 almost 5.2 million people remained unable to vote because of past felony convictions.

Black voters at the ballot box in 1977

Felony convictions make it much more difficult to get jobs and make money. This means a poor person with a felony conviction is more likely to remain poor. Poverty is the strongest predictor of recidivism, or whether someone will commit another crime. This approach to crime makes a cycle that harms Black and poor people. Those stuck in the system have a hard time getting out.

In 1994 President Bill Clinton signed a new crime bill into law. The bill offered money to states that built prisons and cut back on parole. Incarceration rates continued to soar during Clinton's presidency (1993–2001).

The War on Drugs can be compared to the response to the opioid crisis that began in the 1990s. After drug

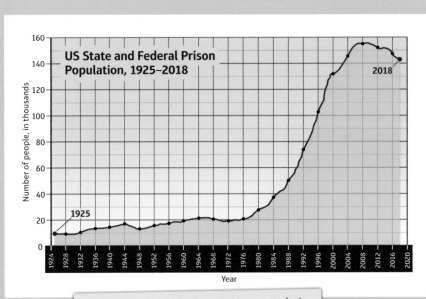

This graph shows how the US prison population began to spike in the 1980s. This is due not to increased crime rates but changes in policy.

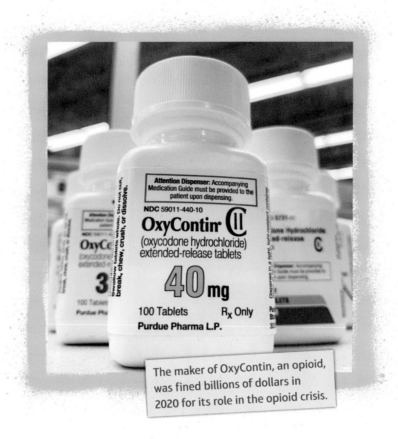

The maker of OxyContin, an opioid, was fined billions of dollars in 2020 for its role in the opioid crisis.

companies lied about how addictive their opioids (a class of pain medications) were, doctors prescribed them too often. Many people became addicted, overdosed, and died. In 2018, 75 percent of opioid deaths were among white people. Those in power handled the crisis differently than they did the War on Drugs. Responses treated addiction like a public health problem, focusing on increasing awareness and expanding access to addiction treatment. The differences suggest that when white people use drugs, they are perceived as victims. But when Black people use drugs, they are seen as criminals.

A school resource officer looks over a school cafeteria.

CHAPTER 3
THE SCHOOL-TO-PRISON PIPELINE

IN 2020, IN RESPONSE TO THE DEATHS OF GEORGE FLOYD, BREONNA TAYLOR, AND OTHERS AT THE HANDS OF POLICE, THE BLACK LIVES MATTER MOVEMENT TOOK TO THE STREETS TO PROTEST AGAINST RACIAL INJUSTICES. Many people called for the removal of school resource officers (SROs) from schools. SROs are police officers tasked with preventing crime in schools and keeping kids safe. But due to lack of funding and resources for mental health and other issues, SROs often have extra responsibilities. One report found that fourteen million students are in schools that have police but no nurse, social worker, or mental health worker. So SROs may respond to student problems for which they do not have training. Activists claimed that SROs contributed to the over-policing of Black children in schools, leading to harsh punishment and even imprisonment.

Protesters in Saint Paul, Minnesota, called for the removal of police officers from schools in 2020.

In the 1990s, many schools adopted zero tolerance policies, resulting in harsh punishments for students who broke rules. Studies show that these punishments are harsher for Black children than for white children, even if the offenses are small. In 2015 a sixteen-year-old named Shakara didn't put her cell phone away quickly enough as class began. In response, an SRO threw her from her desk and dragged her across the floor before charging her with a misdemeanor—a type of crime. The incident revealed to many how disciplinary action could quickly become criminalization in schools.

> ## "We can no longer put a Band-Aid on our nation's preschool-to-prison pipeline, which pushes children out of the education system and criminalizes relatively minor offenses."
>
> —Dr. Tunette Powell, interim director of the UCLA Parent Empowerment Project

Harsh disciplinary action for Black children starts early. Black children make up 18 percent of US preschool students, but 48 percent of children suspended at that age. In 2014 Dr. Tunette Powell recalled telling a group of white mothers that together, her two sons had been suspended eight times. She was surprised to learn that when their children had behaved similarly or worse, their punishment was only a phone call home—no suspensions.

Unequal discipline can start as early as preschool for students of color.

Suspensions and other severe punishments hinder students' academic progress and increase the likelihood that they will drop out of school. One study found that nearly one in four Black male high school dropouts is incarcerated on an average day. And 23 percent of students who are suspended end up in the juvenile justice system. Police presence in schools, unequal disciplinary practices, and the criminalization of Black students all contribute to the school-to-prison pipeline and mass incarceration.

REFLECT

What could schools do to interrupt the school-to-prison pipeline?

Meek Mill in 2018

CHAPTER 4
THE CALL TO ABOLISH PRISONS

IN 2017 RAPPER MEEK MILL WAS ARRESTED AND SENTENCED TO TWO TO FOUR YEARS FOR VIOLATING HIS PROBATION FROM A TEN-YEAR-OLD CONVICTION. His arrest sparked outrage. People around the world got a close look at the injustices in the US criminal justice system. Celebrities such as rapper Jay-Z joined the fight to free people stuck in the system. He helped to found the Reform Alliance to change unfair probation and parole laws.

New laws have helped to reduce US prison populations. In 2010 Congress passed the Fair Sentencing Act, which reduced longer sentences for convictions involving crack cocaine. During the War on Drugs, long sentences for crack cocaine offenses disproportionately impacted Black people.

Black people have been charged at nearly four times the rate of white people under marijuana laws for decades. But as of November 2020, fifteen states and the District of Columbia have legalized marijuana. Twenty-five states and the District of Columbia have removed some of the penalties for marijuana possession.

Jay-Z (*far left*) announces the formation of the Reform Alliance in 2019.

In 2018 President Donald Trump signed the First Step Act to start undoing the damage of unfair sentencing in the US. The law reduced long federal sentences and worked to improve conditions in federal prisons. The act resulted from years of advocacy across political parties.

Some activists are looking away from prisons entirely. Many believe that prisons do little to heal or rehabilitate incarcerated people. They look to programs focusing on restorative justice as an alternative to prison. By using

Protesters rally for prison reform in Jackson, Mississippi, in 2020.

Participants join hands during a peacemaking circle, a method used for restorative justice.

methods such as community service, peacemaking circles, and victim offender dialogues, restorative justice focuses on recognizing and repairing harm. These methods can help to hold offenders directly accountable to their victims.

The fight to end mass incarceration goes on. Activists hope to continue to hold politicians and government leaders accountable to change the US criminal justice system.

REFLECT

When someone hurts you, how do you want them to fix it?

TAKE ACTION

Here are some ways you can help to fight mass incarceration:

Contact your local, state, and national representatives and express your concerns.

Educate yourself about mass incarceration. Check out the Read Woke Reading List on page 30.

Support people in your community affected by incarceration. Ask an adult if you can volunteer your time to help a family experiencing incarceration.

With an adult's help, donate to organizations that help incarcerated people and their families.

Ask an adult if you can get involved with a local restorative justice program.

If you have a friend whose family is dealing with incarceration, ask them what they need. Listen if they want to talk.

TIMELINE

1619: The first enslaved Africans arrive in the Americas.

1865: The first Juneteenth celebrates the end of slavery in the United States.

1877: After Reconstruction ends, states expand convict leasing and Jim Crow laws.

1971: President Nixon states that drug abuse is the greatest challenge facing the US.

1986: President Reagan signs the Anti-Drug Abuse Act, which gives over $1 billion to drug-fighting efforts and expands the number of drug offenses with mandatory minimums.

1994: President Clinton signs the Violent Crime Control and Law Enforcement Act, providing federal funding for more prisons and jails and increasing the amount and length of mandatory prison sentences.

The Gun-Free Schools Act requires students who bring a firearm to school to be suspended for one year and inspires other new zero tolerance policies in schools.

1997: The number of people incarcerated for nonviolent drug offenses hits four hundred thousand, from fifty thousand in 1980.

2010: President Barack Obama signs the Fair Sentencing Act, which reduces longer sentences in crack cocaine cases.

2018: President Trump signs the First Step Act, reducing long federal prison sentences and improving conditions in federal prisons.

GLOSSARY

accountable: required to be responsible for something

black code: a type of law passed after the Civil War that limited the rights of Black people

felony: a serious crime

Jim Crow law: a type of law passed after Reconstruction meant to segregate and disadvantage Black people

mandatory minimum: the minimum amount of prison time for an offense

mass incarceration: imprisoning people in large numbers

parole: conditions under which an inmate may be released early

probation: a sentencing of a period of supervision as an alternative to serving time in prison

recidivism: returning to criminal behavior

zero tolerance: a policy of giving out the most severe punishment to anyone who breaks a rule or law

SOURCE NOTES

8   "The Constitution: Amendments 11-27," National Archives, last reviewed October 14, 2020, https://www.archives.gov /founding-docs/amendments-11-27.

8   Bryan Stevenson, "Slavery Gave America a Fear of Black People and a Taste for Violent Punishment. Both Still Define Our Prison System," *New York Times Magazine*, August 14, 2019, https://www.nytimes.com/interactive/2019/08/14/magazine /prison-industrial-complex-slavery-racism.html.

18   Tunette Powell, "My Son Has Been Suspended Five Times. He's 3," *Washington Post*, July 24, 2014, https://www.washingtonpost .com/posteverything/wp/2014/07/24/my-son-has-been -suspended-five-times-hes-3/.

READ WOKE READING LIST

Beaty, Daniel. *Knock Knock: My Dad's Dream for Me.* New York: Little, Brown, 2013.

The Brennan Center for Justice
https://www.brennancenter.org

Kaba, Mariame. *Missing Daddy.* Chicago: Haymarket Books, 2019.

Marks, Janae. *From the Desk of Zoe Washington.* New York: Katherine Tegen Books, 2020.

Murray, Elizabeth A, PhD. *The Dozier School for Boys: Forensics, Survivors, and a Painful Past.* Minneapolis: Twenty-First Century Books, 2020.

The NAACP Criminal Justice Fact Sheet
https://www.naacp.org/criminal-justice-fact-sheet/

Poole, Hilary W. *Incarceration and Families.* Broomall, PA: Mason Crest, 2017.

Prisons Today Virtual Exhibit Tour
https://interactives.ap.org/2016/prisons-today/

Woodson, Jacqueline. *Visiting Day.* New York: Puffin, 2015.

INDEX

PHOTO ACKNOWLEDGMENTS

Design Elements: Kitch Bain/Shutterstock.com; Ajay Shrivastava/Shutterstock.
com; johnjohnson/Shutterstock.com. Image credits: LightField Studios/
Shutterstock.com, p. 1; Andrey_Popov/Shutterstock.com, p. 4; Creator/
Independent Picture Service, p. 5; Motortion Films/Shutterstock.com, p. 6;
Library of Congress, p. 7; Tippman98x/Shutterstock.com, p. 9; Library of
Congress (LC-D401-16155), pp. 10, 26 (top); AP Photo/Harvey Georges,
pp. 11, 26 (bottom); Contraband Collection/Alamy Stock Photo, p. 12; Science
History Images/Alamy Stock Photo, p. 13; Laura Westlund/Independent
Picture Service, p. 14; PureRadiancePhoto/Shutterstock.com, p. 15; Kate Way/
Shutterstock.com, p. 16; Michael Siluk/Alamy Stock Photo, p. 17; weedezign/
Shutterstock.com, p. 19; AP Photo/Invision/Extra (Portal and Webfeeds), p. 20;
AP Photo/Kathy Willens, p. 21; AP Photo/Rogelio V. Solis, p. 22; AP Photo/
Charles Krupa, p. 23; Kate Way/Shutterstock.com, p. 27. Cecily Lewis portrait
photos by Fernando Decillis.

Cover: Milano Art/Shutterstock.com; LightField Studios/Shutterstock.com.

Content consultant: Dr. Artika R. Tyner, Founder, Planting People Growing Justice

Lerner Publications Company
An imprint of Lerner Publishing Group, Inc.
241 First Avenue North
Minneapolis, MN 55401 USA

For reading levels and more information, look up this title at www.lernerbooks.com.

Main body text set in Aptifer Sans LT Pro.
Typeface provided by Linotype AG.

Designer: Viet Chu

Library of Congress Cataloging-in-Publication Data

Names: Lewis, Cicely, author.
Title: Mass incarceration, Black men, and the fight for justice / Cicely Lewis.
Description: Minneapolis : Lerner Publications, 2022 | Series: Issues in action (Read Woke Books) | Includes bibliographical references and index. | Audience: Ages 9–14 | Audience: Grades 4–6 | Summary: "The US criminal justice system disproportionately targets Black men, resulting in much higher incarceration rates and impacts that can last a lifetime. Readers learn this system's history and context and ways they can help"—Provided by publisher.
Identifiers: LCCN 2020041835 (print) | LCCN 2020041836 (ebook) | ISBN 9781728423425 (library binding) | ISBN 9781728430683 (ebook)
Subjects: LCSH: Imprisonment—Moral and ethical aspects—United States—Juvenile literature. | African American prisoners—Juvenile literature. | Discrimination in criminal justice administration—United States—Juvenile literature. | United States—Race relations—Juvenile literature.
Classification: LCC HV9471 .L47 2022 (print) | LCC HV9471 (ebook) | DDC 365/.608996073—dc23

LC record available at https://lccn.loc.gov/2020041835
LC ebook record available at https://lccn.loc.gov/2020041836

Manufactured in the United States of America
1-49180-49311-2/15/2021